They lived like this in
CHAUCER'S ENGLAND

Author: MARIE NEURATH

Artist: JOHN ELLIS

of the Isotype Institute

FRANKLIN WATTS, INC.,
New York

© 1967 Isotype Institute Limited
Published by Franklin Watts, Inc., 575 Lexington Avenue, New York 22, U.S.A.
Printed in Great Britain by Purnell & Sons, Ltd
Library of Congress Catalog No. 68–10837

CHAUCER'S ENGLAND

Geoffrey Chaucer lived towards the end of the Middle Ages. He was the first great writer of English verse. Before him almost no one wrote in English. The King and his court spoke French, the scholars and church-men used Latin. Although English was the language of everyday life, the books were written in Latin, usually by monks. The Bible was copied again and again and beautifully illustrated. They also made prayer books.

Here we see a scribe at his writing desk. He has a knife for sharpening his quill pen, which he dips in the ink.

In Chaucer's time, Gothic letters were used. Empty spaces at the end of a line were filled in with coloured patterns or elongated figures.

Et exultauerunt filie iude:propter iudicia tua domine

3

The first letter of a new chapter was written large, and decorated.

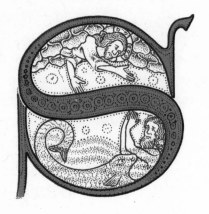

This S encloses two scenes. At the top God is seen extending His hands through the clouds. Below, Jonah is being swallowed by the whale.

Even when a manuscript told stories from the Bible the illustrations showed people of the scribe's own times, so we can see how they lived.

Adam and Eve, expelled from Paradise, had to work for their living. Here are Adam with his spade and Eve with her spindle, just like an English farmer and his wife in those days.

Books like these were written in other countries too. Latin was the common language of all churchmen under the Pope of Rome; bishops, priests, monks and pilgrims moved freely from country to country.

Some books were calendars whose illustrations showed the work of the countryside for each season. This picture is from a book of psalms. It shows a plough being pulled through the heavy soil by four oxen. One man guides the plough while the other drives the animals.

In the next picture the birds are worrying a farmer as he sows his seed. One has alighted on the seedbag itself. Another is trying to take seeds from the ground, but the dog chases it away. When the farmer has harrowed the ground the seeds will be covered by soil.

These men are cutting the corn with sickles,
under the direction of the lord's overseer.
Most farmworkers lived on land which belonged
to a lord or a monastery. They shared common
grazing, and were given strips of farmland
in return for working the lord's farm.

Three horses strain uphill with a cart
laden with sheaves of dry, cut corn.
The men and women push from behind.

The lord had his own mill
where the villagers had to pay
to have their corn ground.
They were not always sure that
they got back the right weight.

This is a windmill.

There were watermills too, like the one in the picture below. We
can see eel-traps in the mill-stream.

Watermills were found useful for other processes besides grinding
corn. In later years many mills were owned by merchants who used
water-power to make goods for sale.

For many centuries the main export from England had been raw wool. The best cloth weavers in Europe wanted English wool. So both lords and villagers kept sheep wherever they could. Sometimes fields were turned over to grazing instead of crops.

This man has bound the sheep's legs together so that he can shear its wool.

From the inland markets merchants took the wool to Calais, a port on the French coast ruled by England. From there it was sold to merchants from other countries.

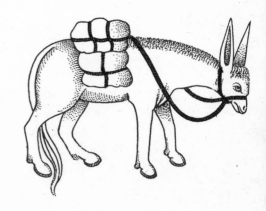

Only the coarser material was made up at home. Many women still used the old hand-spindles, but some had spinning-wheels. The women spun and the men did the weaving.

The weaver in the bottom picture is a woman, but this was unusual.

The finest cloth was made in Flanders. Gradually, Flemish weavers began to settle in England, and they taught their methods to the English craftsmen. The raw wool was now sent by the merchants to villages and homes all over the country, to be made into cloth. Watermills were used for "fulling" or finishing it, and woollen cloth was sold overseas instead of raw wool.

Ships came to England from Flanders and far-away Venice to buy cloth, cheese, coal and tin. They brought luxuries like spices and wine in exchange. Soon the English merchants wanted to carry their goods in their own ships.

Boat builders began to supply them with large ships, able to sail the rough seas.

This picture of a ship shows its elaborate castles at both ends and a topcastle on the mast. The Channel had to be kept free from pirates and other enemies. The merchants expected the King to help them.

The King had no navy. Merchants from the great ports lent him their trading ships to carry soldiers, and special decks were fitted for fighting at sea. The ships had strong bows to ram the enemy.

This is the seal of one of the five most important ports in southern England – the Cinque Ports. It shows the sinking of an enemy ship, one of whose men has fallen into the waves.

The light wooden ships could not carry the heavy cannons which were used on land. Their main weapons were bows and arrows, spears and stones which were hurled down from the topcastle.

During the whole of Chaucer's lifetime England was at war with France. The English King ruled over much of France and tried to extend his power. In the end England lost her French possessions, except Calais.

The English were expert with the longbow, which won them many victories. Their arrows, shot from a distance, could stop even horsemen in armour before they were near enough to use their weapons. Every boy in town and country learned this skill.

Swords and pick-axes were used in attacks on castles. The defenders threw down stones and spears or shot arrows at the enemy through slits in the castle walls.

The knights went into battle in full armour, mounted on strong horses and carrying shields with swords or spears.

In peacetime they showed their skill at tournaments before an audience of knights and ladies.

Knights wooed their ladies with feats of arms. The rules of chivalry taught them bravery, honour and a duty to help the weak.

Many had been to far countries, fighting in France or the Holy Land. Knights from all parts of Europe had joined the crusades to free Palestine from its Saracen rulers. They were attended by squires, young boys who would become knights when they were older.

Special armourers made the heavy shields and armour. In villages all over the country were blacksmiths who shoed the horses.

Hunting deer with horse and hounds was a favourite sport of the King and nobles.

The villagers got extra meat by poaching, which was punished but could not be prevented. They trapped birds, too, by putting sticky lime on a branch, and caught them with a net.

Rabbits were dug out of their warrens or caught in snares. These women are using a ferret to drive them from their holes.

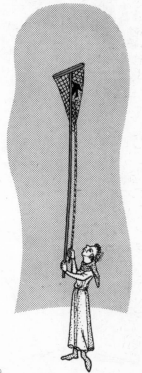

Mounted on their horses, the King and his followers moved from castle to castle. A trail of heavy carts carried the baggage. Ladies were sometimes carried in litters on poles fixed to the saddles of two horses walking one behind the other.

Early castles and monasteries were built on hilltops, or surrounded by moats and walls for protection.

They were strongly built in stone. Here the builders use a pulley and windlass to lift the stones, which will be cut to shape and joined with mortar. Decorations were carved in the stonework.

As the country gradually became more peaceful, open houses with larger windows were built. In cathedrals and churches too, the old heavy walls were replaced by huge windows, and light flooded in, often through coloured glass.

The masons carved strange figures in unexpected places.

They also decorated the churches with exquisite stone carvings, like the grapes and vine leaves on this pillar. Skilled masons were in great demand by churches, kings and nobles. Like all other craftsmen, they belonged to guilds and trained apprentices to become journeymen and then masters.

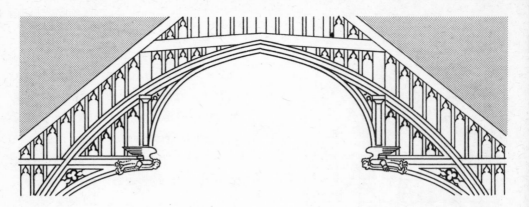

Skilled woodworkers were employed to beautify churches and houses. Halls were built with hammerbeam roofs like this. Separate pieces of wood were used to support one another so that wider structures could be built.

Wooden benches, screens and choir stalls were richly carved. Here is a woodcarver at work.

Like the masons, the woodworkers carved saints and lacy patterns.
But in some places they showed scenes and stories of everyday
life. These were on the underside of hinged choir seats, called
misericords – the Latin word "misericordia" means pity. They were
provided out of sympathy for the priests who had to stand for
hours through the long services: when their seats were up they
could rest on the ledge above the carvings.

The pictures of the boatbuilders and carvers are from misericords,
and here is another, showing the harvest of grapes.
Farmers made wine by treading their own grapes at home.

Wood was used for houses, too.
Cottages had timber frames filled
with clay. The roof beam was
sometimes supported by crucks,
as in this picture. Here the roof
has been widened by adding timbers.

Most houses had neither windows
nor chimneys. Smoke from the
fire escaped through the
rafters or a hole in the roof.
Meat was cured in the smoky
room above the cooking fire.
This man is drying his feet
and shoes near the fire, too.

The great houses had an open fire
in the main hall, and some had
stone chimneys. The lord's
retainers slept in the hall.
At night they cleared away the
benches and tables and lay down
on the rush-covered floor.
The lord and his family had
their own private rooms.

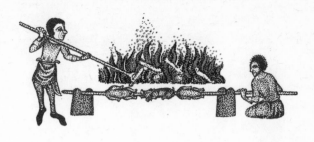

The kitchen was equipped to cook for
many people. Whole joints were roasted
on the spits, and the open fires held
rows of iron saucepans.
Serving men carried the dishes to the
hall, where the lord sat at the high
table with his family and guests.

In the evenings the whole company might sit around to listen to
stories or readings from a book. This would be the duty of the
clergyman who lived there and taught the children their lessons.

Travelling minstrels were welcome guests at the manors and castles. They entertained the company with music, songs and news of other places. Some houses had a special minstrels' gallery in the hall. Musicians also played at the fairs where, for weeks at a time, merchants gathered to buy and sell. There were pipes, gongs and bagpipes, and dancers with bells and drums.

Often a showman with a bear on a lead both amused and frightened the crowds.

This is a Punch and Judy show. Serious plays were staged by the craft guilds. Their stage was a cart which could be moved around the town. They acted stories from the Bible, or morality plays in which good deeds were rewarded and sins punished.

Lyres accompanied
singing at home in
the long dark winter
evenings.
Sacred music was part
of church services
and festivals.

Churches had organs to
lead the singing. This
picture shows an organ
with its pipes. While
the organist plays the
double row of keys his
assistant works the
bellows which pump air
through the pipes.

Besides parish churches served by priests there were monasteries where monks lived and studied. They owned great farms worked by peasants and lay brethren. The early monks had worked the fields themselves, living simply, performing charitable duties, and obeying strict rules. Their day was ordered by the ringing of bells.

But the monasteries became rich, and many churchmen forgot their religious vows, enjoying luxury and wealth. People criticised the clergy, as in this picture which shows a monk, trusted with the keys, helping himself to wine.

Here is a monk sitting in the stocks as punishment for his misdeeds.

Reformers founded new orders of friars who took over the work of the neglectful monks. They lived on charity and wandered from place to place, preaching. Later they settled in friaries, which became as rich as the monasteries.

In those days everyone feared the Day of Judgment, when sinners would suffer hellfire after death. Preachers called for repentance – but some promised lighter punishments or granted pardons to the people who gave them money.

Chaucer, the poet, showed up the greed of pardoners and a dishonest friar in his famous "Canterbury Tales". This book is about a group of pilgrims who tell stories on their way to Canterbury Cathedral.

Many clergymen still did good work in the hospitals and schools. Any clever boy, rich or poor, could be admitted to the church grammar schools. Teaching was in Latin. The boys were kept at lessons all day, and were severely punished if they did not work.

Released from the classroom, they could play games like spinning the top or pretending to be knights jousting in a tournament.

From school a boy could go to the university.

Oxford was the first university in England. Cambridge followed soon afterwards. Students living in lodgings in the town were unruly, so colleges were set up where they could live under supervision.

The teachers were mostly trained clergy.

But some of the teachers spent their time in study rather than religious work. It was here, during Geoffrey Chaucer's lifetime, that other men began to write books in English. Amongst them was John Wycliffe, a courageous teacher who led a movement for the reform of the Church. His class was closed, so he retired to a country parish where he translated the Bible into English.

Law was now taught at the Inns of Court in London, and its teachers were no longer clergymen. Medicine was not taught at university. It was not a science. Physicians had some useful medicines, but they mixed strange ingredients and their treatments relied on magic and the position of the stars in the sky.

Here are some pictures of patients. One has to inhale fumes from a boiling pot, another is having drops in his ear, while the third is being told how to treat his skin disease.

Chaucer was less than 10 years old when Europe was terror-stricken
by the outbreak of an unknown disease which killed millions of people
in every country, including Britain. It was called the Black Death,
and no one knew what caused it. Innocent people were accused of
spreading it. Doctors were helpless, and the monks and nuns who ran
the hospitals could not cope with the thousands of patients.

The disease died out after a long series of outbreaks.
Much later it was discovered that fleas which live on black rats
carry this plague, and it could then be controlled.

The death of so many people upset the life of the countryside. Land
lay vacant, and the landowners could not get workers. Those who
remained asked for higher wages, and moved away if they did not get
them. Small farmers bought more land and employed labourers. Many
people were now paid in money, and wages rose. When the King made
laws to stop this, and the landowners tried to enforce the old ways,
the peasants became discontented and rebelled. They were promised
better conditions but the King broke his promise and executed their
leaders. However, the old system could not be restored.

Some farm workers went to the towns, where they had more freedom and earned wages. Here the guildmasters had ruled for many years. They saw to it that the work was of good quality, supervised training and fixed prices. They protected the town and called the people to work in the fields which belonged to the town.

Here a stone mason and a carpenter show their work to a guildmaster dressed in his ceremonial robes.

At one time every journeyman became a master when he was trained. Now the masters, guarding their own privileges, made this almost impossible. The journeymen who could not become masters were a new working class. Some clothiers went into the country and established an industry there, to escape the town regulations.

Some masters gave up their craft to become merchants who bought and sold goods made by others. They grew rich and the country prospered.

Cloth was exported and luxuries were imported. The English copied the elegant foreign fashions.

This well-dressed merchant is giving alms to a beggar in rags.

It was no longer necessary for the King to ask foreign bankers for a loan. Now English merchants lent money to the King, who gave their towns freedom and other rights in return.

London, the centre of trade and commerce, grew rapidly.

31

No town in England had so many churches as the City of London. Though the largest of the English cities, it was still small compared with Paris and the flourishing towns of Flanders and Italy, because Southern Europe had a long history of contact with ancient civilisations. But when ships crossed the oceans and discovered new lands, Britain, on the edge of the Atlantic, was in a favourable position.

After the Middle Ages, British ships and merchants travelled to far countries, and people all over the world came to use English, the language which grew through the writings of Wycliffe and Chaucer.